SCIENCE EXPLORER

SEARCHING THE SKY

Follow the Clues

by Tamra B. Orr

CHERRY LAKE PUBLISHING · ANN ARBOR, MICHIGAN

CHERRY LAKE Publishing

Published in the United States of America by Cherry Lake Publishing
Ann Arbor, Michigan
www.cherrylakepublishing.com

CONTENT EDITOR: Melissa Miller, Next Generation Science Standards Writer; Science Teacher, Farmington, Arkansas
BOOK DESIGN AND ILLUSTRATION: The Design Lab
READING ADVISER: Marla Conn, ReadAbility, Inc.

PHOTO CREDITS: Cover and page 1, ©solarseven/Shutterstock, Inc.; page 4, ©Krasowit/Shutterstock; page 5, ©Victor Fernandez/Shutterstock, Inc.; page 6, ©Sergey Kamshylin/Shutterstock, Inc.; page 7, ©Dennis van de Water/Shutterstock, Inc.; page 8, ©kavring/Shutterstock, Inc.; pages 9 and 14, ©Triff/Shutterstock, Inc.; page 10, ©I. Pilon/Shutterstock, Inc.; page 11, ©Africa Studio/Shutterstock, Inc.; page 12, ©Alix Kreil/Shutterstock, Inc.; page 13, ©samsam62/Shutterstock, Inc.; page 15, ©Nuttapong/Shutterstock, Inc.; page 16, ©Ivancovlad/Shutterstock, Inc.; page 17, ©Grigoryeva Liubov Dmitrievna/Shutterstock, Inc.; page 18, ©JEFF SMITH/Alamy; page 19, ©Karol Kozlowski/Shutterstock, Inc.; page 21, ©Monkey Business Images/Shutterstock, Inc.; page 22, ©bikeriderlondon/Shutterstock, Inc.; page 23, ©Balefire/Shutterstock, Inc.; page 24, ©ChinellatoPhoto/Shutterstock, Inc.; page 25, ©Galyna Andrushko/Shutterstock, Inc.; page 26, ©michaeljung/Shutterstock, Inc.; page 27, ©racorn/Shutterstock, Inc.; page 28, ©michaeljung/Shutterstock, Inc.; page 29, ©Aina Jameela/Shutterstock, Inc.

LIBRARY OF CONGRESS CATALOGING-IN-PUBLICATION DATA
Orr, Tamra, author.
  Searching the sky / by Tamra Orr.
    pages cm. — (Science explorer) (Follow the clues)
  Audience: Grades 4 to 6.
  Summary: "Use the next generation science standards to learn how meteorites are identified." — Provided by publisher.
  Includes bibliographical references and index.
  ISBN 978-1-62431-782-8 (lib. bdg.) — ISBN 978-1-62431-792-7 (pbk.) — ISBN 978-1-62431-812-2 (ebook) — ISBN 978-1-62431-802-3 (pdf)
  1. Meteorites—Juvenile literature. 2. Meteors—Juvenile literature. I. Title.

QB755.2.O77 2014
523.5'1—dc23   2013045709

Cherry Lake Publishing would like to acknowledge the work of The Partnership for 21st Century Skills.
Please visit www.p21.org for more information.

Printed in the United States of America, Corporate Graphics Inc.
January 2014

This book is intended to introduce readers to the Next Generation Science Standards (NGSS). These standards emphasize a general set of eight practices for scientific investigation, rather than a rigid set of steps. Keywords taken from the NGSS are highlighted in the text. The eight science practices are:
1. Asking questions
2. Developing and using models
3. Planning and carrying out investigations
4. Analyzing and interpreting data
5. Using mathematics and computational thinking
6. Constructing explanations
7. Engaging in argument from evidence
8. Obtaining, evaluating, and communicating information

TABLE OF CONTENTS

CHAPTER 1

STREAKING ACROSS THE SKY

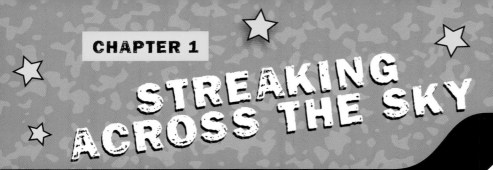

A meteor can appear as a streak of light as it travels through Earth's atmosphere.

"Wait, say it again. Your dad is a met . . . meteor . . . a what?" asked Samantha.

Tomiko grinned. It was not the first time someone had asked her this exact question. Her father was a meteoricist (mee-tee-OR-ih-cist), a scientist who studies **meteors**. Very few people had ever heard of the word. Tomiko thought it was one of the most fascinating jobs in the world.

Dr. Nakata examined the meteors that fell all the way from outer space to the ground. This helped him determine clues about how old the solar system is and what planets are made of.

"He is a meteoricist," said Tomiko slowly. "He looks at the chunks of iron and metal that land on the earth. He finds out what they can tell science about how the universe was formed." She was proud of her dad and what he did. She was also excited because tomorrow Dr. Nakata was taking Tomiko and Samantha to the country to catch a glimpse of the Perseid meteor shower. This incredible meteor shower is visible for a few days every summer.

Rural areas, far from city lights, are the best places to see stars and meteor showers.

The next night, just as it was beginning to get dark, Dr. Nakata, Tomiko, and Samantha headed out to a wilderness area where there were no bright city lights to block their view of the meteors.

"This is going to be so cool!" Tomiko said as she and Samantha unfolded lawn chairs in the center of an open, grassy area.

"I looked up some pictures of meteor showers online before we left," Samantha said. "They were beautiful!"

"The view will be even better in person," Dr. Nakata replied.

The girls could barely contain themselves as they waited for the meteors to come into view. Finally, just as they were starting to fall asleep in their chairs, Dr. Nakata shouted out, "Here they come!"

Some stargazers use a telescope for a closer look at meteor showers.

Perseid meteor showers take place every summer.

"Whoa!" Tomiko yelled as streaks of light began shooting across the night sky. Samantha jumped out of her chair in excitement. Dr. Nakata snapped photos and took notes in a small notebook as they watched the meteors fall. After about 45 minutes, the show was over. The girls helped Dr. Nakata pack up their things before piling into the car to head home.

Even though it was late and they were very tired, Tomiko and Samantha could not stop talking about the meteor shower on the way back. They were still discussing it when they pulled into the Nakatas' driveway. On the way into the house, Samantha's toe bumped into something on the ground. "Ouch!" she said, rubbing the top of her foot.

It can take careful study to tell whether a rock is a meteorite.

"Look!" Tomiko shouted, pointing at the ground where Samantha had stumbled. "That rock wasn't there earlier."

Samantha looked back at her friend. "Do you think ...?"

"It could be a **meteorite**!" Tomiko jumped up and down at the possibility.

"Interesting," said Dr. Nakata. "That's a question worth investigating!"

ALL ABOUT METEORS

Meteors heat up as they move through Earth's atmosphere.

Meteors are chunks of rock and metal that have broken off from larger objects in space. Most of them are pieces of **asteroids**. Others break off moons or planets. They fly through space, and eventually some of them end up on a collision course with Earth. As they fly through Earth's **atmosphere**, they heat up to incredible temperatures, leaving behind bright trails of light. This heat also causes most meteors to disintegrate before they ever reach Earth's surface.

Meteors that do reach the surface are called meteorites. By the time they hit the ground, they have cooled off and are no longer surrounded by burning light. Most are very small. However, larger ones hit the ground with enough force to form **craters**.

CHAPTER 2

A CLOSER LOOK

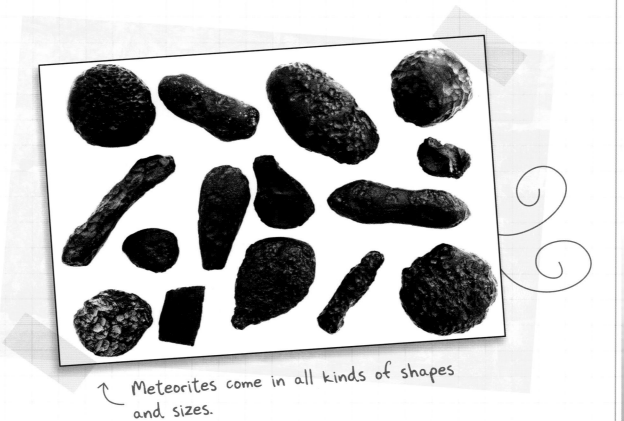

Meteorites come in all kinds of shapes and sizes.

The next day, Dr. Nakata brought the girls and the rock they had discovered to his lab. "I can't wait to test this rock and find out if it's a meteorite," Tomiko said as she burst through the laboratory doors.

Dr. Nakata smiled. "Slow down, Tomiko. It's good to be excited, but first you're going to need some more information about meteors."

Scientists start their investigations by learning as much as they can about a topic.

"How will we find the information we need?" asked Samantha.

"I have some real meteorite samples you can see," said Dr. Nakata. "You can also use these books and go online using my computer. I'll be around if you have any questions."

Dr. Nakata headed off to work on a project of his own, and the girls began reading all they could find about different kinds of meteorites. They also looked at a row of meteorites that Dr. Nakata laid out for them on one of the lab's metal worktables.

"There sure are a lot of different kinds of meteorites," said Samantha. "They come in all sorts of shapes and sizes. How are we going

to figure out if our rock is a meteorite when there are so many types to compare it to?"

"They might all look a little different," Tomiko replied, "but this article I found online says that there are certain things that most meteorites have in common."

"That's great news," said Samantha. "Maybe we can use that information to make a plan for testing our rock."

Tomiko and Samantha made plenty of notes as they collected research.

A computer is a great tool for storing and sorting information.

Tomiko tapped her pen against her lips as she concentrated on the information in front of her. After a few moments, her face lit up. "I've got it!" she said. "We can come up with a list of features that meteorites have. Then we can turn that into a checklist on the computer and go through each step to see if it matches our rock."

"Perfect," Samantha replied. "That is sure to tell us if this rock really did fall from outer space."

"Let's get started right away!" Tomiko shouted, already typing away furiously on Dr. Nakata's laptop.

EXAMINING METEORITES

Meteorites provide infor-
mation about Earth and
the surrounding universe.

Meteorites are a valuable source of information for **astronomers** and other scientists who want to learn more about outer space. Meteorites can come from faraway planets, moons, and asteroids. It can take years to launch a successful space mission to study these objects. Meteorites allow scientists to research these faraway places without ever leaving home.

Meteorites also provide scientists with a glimpse into the past. Many of the meteorites are chunks of objects that formed millions of years ago. By studying them, scientists can get evidence of how our own planet was formed and what the universe was like before humans were around to study it.

CHAPTER 3

COMPARING AND CALCULATING

↖ The dents on this meteorite are called regmaglypts.

"Okay," said Tomiko. "What things should we include on our checklist?"

"Well, it says here that meteorites have a melted outer layer because they get really hot when they pass through Earth's atmosphere," Samantha said, pointing to a passage in one of Dr. Nakata's books. "Some of them are also covered in shapes called regmaglypts. They look like thumbprints. Look, you can see them here on this meteorite." Samantha held up one of Dr. Nakata's samples.

↰ A meteorite that is magnetic attracts metal, just like any other magnet.

Tomiko typed Samantha's suggestions into the checklist. "I read earlier that you can often see shiny streaks or spots of metal when you break a meteorite open," Tomiko said. "I'll add that one, too."

"Oh, that's right!" Samantha said. "I saw online that meteorites are usually **magnetic** because of the metal in them."

"Anything else?" Tomiko asked.

"This book says that meteorites have higher **density** than regular Earth rocks," Samantha said.

"I'm not sure how to test that, but we can ask my dad," said Tomiko. "I think that should be enough. Let's start testing this rock!"

"First, let's look at the outside," said Samantha. "It's pretty smooth, but I don't know if I'd say that it's melted."

Tomiko held up two of Dr. Nakata's meteorites. "It doesn't quite look like either of these. Then again, these two look a lot different from each other."

"Do you think we should mark that column as 'maybe'?" Samantha asked.

"Good idea," said Tomiko. "We can come back to that one if we need a tiebreaker!"

Samantha ran her hands across the surface of their rock. "I think we can put a 'no' in the regmaglypts column," she said. "It has little markings, but they are way smaller than the ones on your dad's meteorite."

"Okay," said Tomiko. "Let's find a magnet and see if it sticks."

↰ Sometimes, it takes a very close inspection to compare one rock to another.

"There's one on this table," Samantha said. She tried sticking it to the rock, but it fell to the floor.

"See if it sticks to my dad's meteorite samples," Tomiko suggested.

Samantha tried the magnet on three different meteorites, and it stuck to all three of them. "Well, I guess we know our rock isn't magnetic," she said.

"That's okay," said Tomiko as she typed the results into their file. "Let's ask my dad to break the rock open so we can look at the inside."

Most meteorites contain iron or an iron-nickel combination. This makes the meteorites magnetic.

A tool like a rock hammer can split open rocks for further study.

The girls knocked on the door of the room where Dr. Nakata was working and asked him to help with the last steps of their project. He grabbed some tools from a nearby box and easily split their rock into two chunks.

Tomiko and Samantha leaned over to get a close look at the inside of their rock.

"Hmm," said Samantha. "Do you see any metal pieces?"

"These parts are kind of shiny, but they don't really look like the photos we saw online," Tomiko answered.

"You're right," said Samantha. "Let's mark it as a 'no.'"

"Okay," said Tomiko. "On to figuring out density, our last step!"

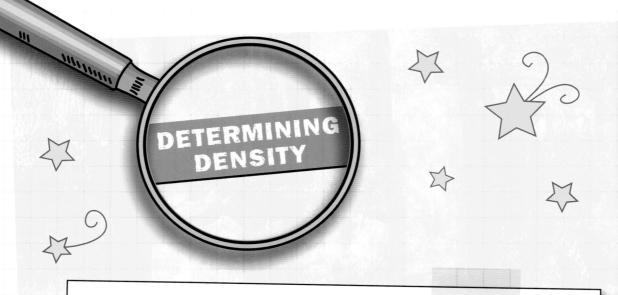

DETERMINING DENSITY

You can calculate density by taking measurements and doing simple math. Density is a measurement of how much **mass** is packed into a certain **volume**. Once you know the mass and volume of an object, you can easily figure out its density.

How do you figure out mass and volume? Mass is easy to figure out. All you need to do is weigh the object on a scale. Volume is a little more complicated. You need a measuring container with milliliters (ml) marked on the side. The container must be large enough to hold the object you are measuring. Fill the container partway with water and use the markings on the side of the glass to measure how many milliliters the water takes up. Now drop your object into the water. Look to see where the water level is now. Subtract your first measurement from this number. The result is your object's volume.

density = mass/volume

CHAPTER 4

METEORITE OR REGULAR ROCK?

← Going back over all of the data you collected can make it easier to form a conclusion.

Dr. Nakata walked over to where the girls were working. He peered over their shoulders at the charts and notes they had created. "How is your investigation coming along?" he asked. "Have you discovered if your rock is actually a meteorite?"

"It's going great!" said Tomiko. "I think we might finally have enough information to solve this mystery. All we have to do is look over our **data** and come up with an explanation."

Samantha and Tomiko made sure to double-check all of their math.

The girls set their rock on the table next to the meteorite samples and started going over their checklist from the top.

"Well," said Samantha, "we didn't really have a solid answer about the melted outer layer, our first step. So let's skip that one for now."

"The next step was to look for regmaglypts," said Tomiko. "Our rock didn't have them."

"Both of the next steps were to see if there was any metal in the rock," Samantha continued. "It wasn't magnetic, and we didn't see anything on the inside."

"And according to our calculations, the rock's density is way lower than the meteorites we measured," Tomiko added. "I guess that pretty much explains it, then. Our rock is just a regular old rock!"

"Yep," Samantha agreed. "I guess we don't need to use the first step as a tiebreaker after all!"

"I suspected this would be the result," said Dr. Nakata. "I hope you girls aren't disappointed."

"No way!" Tomiko shouted. "This was so much fun! I loved looking at the meteorites you have here and reading about how meteors are formed."

"Totally," Samantha said. "I want to learn even more about meteors now!"

Dr. Nakata smiled at the girls' reactions. "You're welcome back in the lab anytime!" he said.

 Meteors can be an exciting topic to study.

MAJOR METEORITES

Allende meteorite

Thousands of meteorites land on Earth every year. It is very difficult to measure exactly how many there are, though. This is because most of them are as small as specks of dust. Many are so small that they burn up before making it all the way down to the surface! However, some are much larger. Scientists study these meteorites carefully to see what they can learn about outer space. Here are some famous meteorites that have crash-landed on Earth:

☆ The Allende Meteorite: Broken pieces of the Allende meteorite crash-landed in northern Mexico in February 1969. These pieces ranged in size from tiny fragments to huge stones that weighed hundreds of pounds. Altogether, the meteorite material discovered by scientists weighed more than 1 ton. Some parts of the meteorite are more than 4.5 billion years old! By studying them, scientists have learned valuable new things about the way our solar system was formed.

☆ The First Moon Meteorite: In 1981, scientists discovered a new meteorite in Antarctica. After performing some tests, they learned that it came from Earth's moon. Before that, scientists had believed that all meteors were pieces of asteroids.

☆ The Hoba Meteorite: Discovered in the African nation of Namibia, the Hoba meteorite is the largest ever discovered in one piece. It weighs around 66 tons, making it too heavy to move from its original location!

 Hoba meteorite

CHAPTER 5

SHOW-AND-TELL

↖ It can be scary to do a presentation in front of a class—but it can be exciting, too!

A few days later, Tomiko and Samantha brought their rock to school for the class's show-and-tell day. They also borrowed one of Dr. Nakata's real meteorite samples to take along. The two girls were excited to share what they had learned with their classmates.

Everyone was excited to see a real-life meteorite!

Samantha passed the meteorite and the regular rock around the room for the students to examine. Tomiko explained how they had gone to see the meteor shower the previous week and found their rock afterward. Then Samantha talked about the way they had researched meteorites and tested the rock to see if it had fallen from the sky or had formed right here on Earth.

Tomiko explained that they had looked for regmaglypts, checked the rock's density, and checked for magnetism. She showed her classmates the regmaglypts on the meteorite and pointed out how there weren't

any on their rock. She also showed how the meteorite was magnetic and the rock was not.

"Even though our rock was just a rock, we learned a lot about meteorites," said Samantha.

"So if we ever do find a real meteorite, we'll know exactly what to look for to identify it correctly!" Tomiko added.

Their teacher, Mr. Owens, started clapping, and the rest of the class joined in. Samantha laughed as Tomiko bowed to their audience. "Who knew that looking at rocks could be so exciting?" Samantha asked.

"I don't know, but I can't wait to look at more!" Tomiko answered.

Mr. Owens was proud of his students.

ADJUSTING FOR AN AUDIENCE

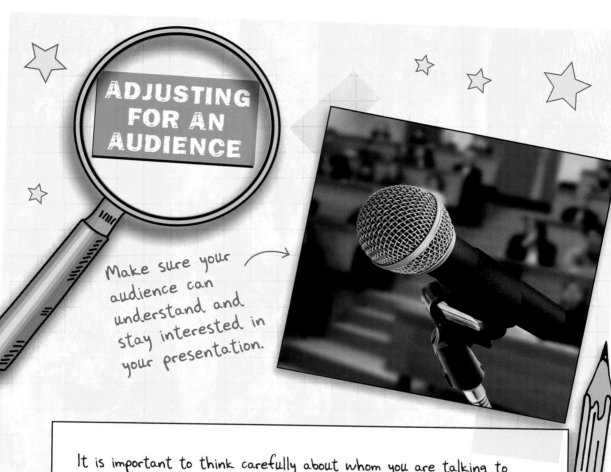

Make sure your audience can understand and stay interested in your presentation.

It is important to think carefully about whom you are talking to when presenting your findings. For example, you might share information differently with your classmates than you would with your teacher. Your classmates might not have studied the topic you are discussing. So you will want to fill them in on any background information they need to understand your investigation. Your teacher would probably already know about your subject, so you can skip the basics and get down to the main points. You can also discuss scientific details with your teacher that your classmates might not understand or be interested in. Always keep your audience in mind when you are preparing to present your findings.

GLOSSARY

asteroids (AS-tuh-roidz) small, rocky objects that travel around the sun

astronomers (uh-STRAH-nuh-mehrz) scientists who study stars, planets, and space

atmosphere (AT-muhs-feer) the mixture of gases that surrounds a planet

craters (KRAY-turz) holes caused by one object in space hitting another

data (DAY-tuh) information collected in a place so that something can be done with it

density (DEN-sih-tee) the amount of matter in an object

magnetic (mag-NET-ik) acting like or including a magnet

mass (MAS) the amount of physical matter that an object contains

meteorite (MEE-tee-uh-rite) a piece of rock from space that falls to the earth

meteors (MEE-tee-urz) pieces of rock or metal from space that speed into the earth's atmosphere and form a streak of light as they burn and fall to Earth

volume (VAHL-yoom) the amount of space taken up by a three-dimensional object, such as a box, or by a substance within a container

BOOKS

Kelley, J. A. *Meteor Showers*. New York: Children's Press, 2010.

Parker, Steve. *Space Objects: Comets, Asteroids, and Meteors*. New York: Rosen Central, 2007.

Vogt, Gregory. *Meteors and Comets*. Minneapolis: Lerner, 2010.

WEB SITES

Meteor Crater

www.meteorcrater.com

Learn more about the 50,000-year-old crater in Northern Arizona.

Museum of Natural History: Meteorites

www.nhm.ac.uk/kids-only/earth-space/meteorites

Learn more about meteorites at this Natural History Museum site.

INDEX

ABOUT THE AUTHOR

Tamra B. Orr is an author living in the Pacific Northwest. Orr has a degree in secondary education and English from Ball State University. She is the mother of four and the author of more than 350 books for readers of all ages. When she isn't writing or reading books, she is writing letters to friends all over the world. Although fascinated by all aspects of science, most of her current scientific method skills are put to use tracking down lost socks, missing keys, and overdue library books.